MW01537195

Sarah Retter

CHINA: CHINESE TRAVEL PHRASES for ENGLISH SPEAKING TRAVELERS

The 1.000 phrases you need to be understood when traveling in China

© 2015 by Sarah Retter
© 2015 by UNITEXTO

All rights reserved

Published by UNITEXTO

UNITEXTO
Digital Publishing

Table of Contents

1.

Bank
银行

1.1.

I want to make a withdrawal
我想要取现

1.2.

Could you give me some smaller notes?
能给我一些小面额的纸币吗?

1.3.

I'd like to pay this in, please
我想存入这个，谢谢

1.4.

How many days will it take for the check to clear?
这张支票过户需要几天时间?

1.5.

Can the passport serve as an ID?
护照可以起身份证的作用吗?

1.6.

Here's my ID card
这是我的身份证

1.7.

I'd like to transfer some money to this account
我想往这个账户里面转一些钱

1.8.

Could you transfer ... from my current account
to my deposit account?
你能......从我现在的账户往我的存款账户转账
吗?

1.9.

I'd like to open an account
我想开户

1.10.

I'd like to open a personal account
我想开一个个人账户

1.11.

Can I open a business account?
我能开一个企业账户吗?

1.12.

Could you tell me my balance, please?
你能告诉我我的余额吗，谢谢?

1.13.

Could I have a statement, please?
我能要一张清单吗，谢谢?

1.14.

I'd like to change some money
我想兑换一些钱

1.15.

I'd like to order some foreign currency
我想订一些外币

1.16.

What's the exchange rate for euros?
对欧元的汇率是多少?

1.17.

I'd like to exchange euros to dollars
我想把欧元换成美元

1.18.

Could I order a new checkbook, please?
我想要一个新的支票簿，谢谢?

1.19.

I'd like to cancel a check
我想取消一个支票

1.20.

I'd like to cancel this standing order
我想取消这个委托书

1.21.

Where's the nearest cash machine?
最近的自动取款机在哪里?

1.22.

What's the interest rate on this account?
这个账户的利率是多少?

1.23.

What's the current interest rate for personal
loans?
现在个人贷款的利率是多少?"

1.24.

I've lost my bank card

我丢了我的银行卡

1.25.

I want to report a lost card

我想挂失卡

1.26.

I think my card has been stolen

我想我的卡被偷了

1.27.

We've got a joint account

我们有一个共同账户

1.28.

I'd like to tell you about a change of address

我想说一下地址的变更

1.29.

I've forgotten my Internet banking password

我忘记了我的网银密码

1.30.

I've forgotten the PIN number for my card

我忘记了我的信用卡密码

1.31.

I'll have a new one sent out to you

我会给你发送一个新的

1.32.

Could I make an appointment to see the

manager?

我可以预约见经理吗?

1.33.

I'd like to speak to someone about a mortgage

我想谈一笔抵押贷款

2. Bar

酒吧

2.1.

Bring me a beer

给我一个啤酒

2.2.

Two beers, please

两个啤酒

2.3.

Three shots of tequila, please

三个龙舌兰，谢谢

2.4.

I would like a glass of wine

我想要一杯葡萄酒

2.5.

I'll have the same, please

我要一样的，谢谢

2.6.

Nothing for me, thank you

我什么都不要，谢谢

2.7.

I'll pay for everyone

都由我付账

2.8.

Another round, please

请再来一轮

2.9.

Are you still serving drinks?

你还提供饮料吗?

2.10.

Do you have any snacks?

你有零食吗?

2.11.

Do you have any sandwiches?

你有三明治吗?

2.12.

Do you serve food?

你提供食物吗?

2.13.

What time does the kitchen close?

厨房什么时候关门?

2.14.

Are you still serving food?

你们还提供食物吗?

2.15.

What sort of sandwiches do you have?

你们有什么种类的三明治?

2.16.

Do you have any hot food?

你有什么热食?

2.17.

Could we see a menu, please?

我能看一下菜单吗，谢谢?

2.18.

Can I smoke inside?

我能在里面抽烟吗?

2.19.

Do you mind if I smoke?

我可以抽烟吗?

2.20.

Would you like a cigarette?

要抽烟吗?

2.21.

Have you got a light?

你有灯吗?

3. Boutique

精品店

3.1.

Could I try this on?
我可以试穿这个吗?

3.2.

Could I try these shoes on?
我能试穿这双鞋子吗?

3.3.

I need the size ...
我想要......号

3.4.

Do you have these shoes in size ...?
你有......号的这种鞋子吗?

3.5.

Do you have the trousers in size ...?
你有......号的这条裤子吗?

3.6.

Do you have a fitting room?
你有试衣间吗?

3.7.

Where's the fitting room?
试衣间在哪里?

3.8.

Have you got this in a smaller size?
你有小号的这个吗?

3.9.

Have you got this in a larger size?

你有大号的这个吗?

3.10.

Does this fit me??

这个合适吗?

3.11.

The shirt is too big, I don't like it

这件衬衫太大，我不喜欢

3.12.

The pants are too small, I can't fit in them

裤子太小了，我穿不合适

3.13.

I need some high heels, can you help me?

我想要一些高跟鞋，你能帮助我吗?

3.14.

Do you have this sweater in another color?

你有其他颜色的这种运动衫吗?

3.15.

What material is this made of?

这是什么材料的?

3.16.

Can I wash this skirt at home?

我能在家洗这件裙子吗?

3.17.

Does this suit require dry-cleaning?

这件西装需要干洗吗?

3.18.

Can I use the fitting room?
我可以用试衣间吗**?**

4.

Bus travel
乘坐公共汽车

4.1.

Where can I buy tickets?
我在哪里买车票**?**

4.2.

I need one child return ticket
我要一张儿童返程票

4.3.

Where's the ticket office?
售票处在哪里**?**

4.4.

What time's the next bus to ...?
下一班去......的公共汽车是几点钟**?**

4.5.

Can I buy a ticket on the bus?
我可以在公共汽车上买票吗**?**

4.6.

I'd like a return to ..., coming back on Sunday
我想回......星期天回来

4.7.

Where do I change for ...?
去......我在哪里换乘?

4.8.

Can I have a timetable, please?
能给我一张时刻表吗，谢谢?

4.9.

How often do the buses run to ...?
去......的公共汽车多久一班?

4.10.

The bus is running late
公共汽车晚点了

4.11.

The bus has been cancelled
这班公共汽车取消了

4.12.

Does this bus stop at ...?
这个公共汽车在......停吗?

4.13.

Could you tell me when we get to ...?
能告诉我我们什么时候到......吗?

4.14.

Is this seat taken?
这个座位有人吗?

4.15.

Do you mind if I sit here?

我坐可以吗**?**

4.16.

I've lost my ticket. What should I do?

我的票丢了。我该怎么办**?**

4.17.

What time do we arrive in …?

我们几点钟到**……?**

4.18.

What's this stop?

这是哪一站**?**

4.19.

What's the next stop?

下一站是哪里**?**

4.20.

This is my stop. Can you let me get off?

我到站了。能让我下车吗**?**

4.21.

I'm getting off here. Could you please move a bit?

我在下车。你能往前开一点吗**?**

4.22.

How many stops is it to …?

到**……**有几站**?**

4.23.

How much is the ticket to ...?

到......的票多少钱?

4.24.

Where is the bus station, please?

请问公共汽车站在哪里?

4.25.

When does the bus leave for...?

到......的公共汽车几点开?

4.26.

How many stops before...?

到......之前有多少站?

5. Business meetings
商务会面

5.1.

I would like to schedule a meeting with you

我想约你会面

5.2.

Are you available next week?

你下周有时间吗?

5.3.

Can I reschedule our meeting?

我可以重新定会面的时间吗?

5.4.

I'll call you in the morning to confirm the time

我早上会打电话确认时间

5.5.

When should we arrive?

我们应该什么时候到?

5.6.

Where's the event going to happen?

会有什么事情发生?

5.7.

Are there going to be some presentations?

¿Van a haber presentaciones?

5.8.

Who is presenting tonight?

¿Quién estará presentando esta noche?

5.9.

What's this girl's name?

那个女孩叫什么?

5.10.

Can you please introduce us?

请你介绍我们认识好吗?

5.11.

Who is the guy in the corner?

角落里的那个小子是谁?

5.12.

Do you know the man in the gray suit?

你认识那个穿灰色西装的男人吗**?**

5.13.

What's your last name?

你贵姓**?**

5.14.

Can I get your business card?

能给我一张你的名片吗**?**

5.15.

Could you write down your number, please?

请把你的名字写下来**?**

5.16.

Can we talk about the job now?

现在我们能谈论一下这个工作吗**?**

5.17.

I would like to see your boss

我想见你的老板

5.18.

Can I speak to your mentor?

我能和你的导师谈谈吗**?**

5.19.

This is my associate, Mr. ...

这是我的助理，**......**先生

5.20.

I hope your secretary gave you my message

我希望你的秘书把我的消息给了你

5.21.

Should we get out of the office and go for a lunch?

我们应该离开办公室去吃午饭吗?

5.22.

What do you think about my proposal?

你觉得我的建议怎么样?

5.23.

I would like to know your opinion

我想知道你的意见

5.24.

I wanted to ask you for an advice

我想问一下你的建议

5.25.

I want to talk about investing in my company

我想谈一下在我的公司里投资

6. Coffee

咖啡

6.1.

Can I get a coffee?

我想要一杯咖啡?

6.2.

I'll have a coffee, please

我想要一杯咖啡，谢谢

6.3.

An orange juice for me, please

给我一杯桔子汁，谢谢

6.4.

Bring me a tea

给我一杯茶

6.5.

Do you have frappes?

你有冰镇的吗?

6.6.

Double espresso with cream, please

两份浓咖啡加奶油，谢谢

6.7.

Can I have a macchiato?

我想要玛奇朵?

6.8.

Just a glass of water for me

给我一杯水就行了

6.9.

I'll have a hot chocolate

我要一个巧克力热饮

6.10.

Do you have any fresh juice?

你有新鲜的果汁吗**?**

6.11.

Have you got lemonade?

你有柠檬水吗**?**

6.12.

I've already ordered

我已经点了

6.13.

How much do I owe you?

我欠你多少**?**

6.14.

Keep the change!

不用找零了**!**

6.15.

Do you have internet access here?

你有网络吗**?**

6.16.

Do you have wireless internet here?

你有无线网络吗**?**

6.17.

What's theWi-Fi password?

Wi-Fi 密码是多少**?**

6.18.

Can you move my drink, I'll sit outside
能移动一下我的饮料吗，我想坐外面

6.19.

Where is the restroom?
洗手间在哪里?

6.20.

Do you serve alcoholic drinks?
你有酒吗?

6.21.

What kind of tea do you have?
你有什么茶?

7.

Car accidents
车祸

7.1.

Can you call the police?
你能叫警察吗?

7.2.

I have a flat tire, can you call help?
我的车胎漏气了，你能打电话求助吗?

7.3.

I'm out of gas, is there any gas station near?
我没有油了，附件有加油站吗?

7.4.

My breaks aren't working, what should I do?
我的刹车失灵了，我应该怎么办**?**

7.5.

There was a major collision, what happened?
有一个大的碰撞，怎么了**?**

7.6.

I'm hurt, can you call the ambulance?
我受伤了，你能叫救护车吗**?**

7.7.

Is doctor on his way?
有医生来吗**?**

7.8.

Did you see the car coming?
你看到来的车了吗**?**

7.9.

Where is the nearest hospital?
最近的医院在哪里**?**

7.10.

Is the ambulance coming?
救护车来了吗**?**

7.11.

Do you have a first aid kit?
你有急救箱吗**?**

7.12.

Am I getting a ticket?
我会收到罚单吗?

7.13.

Did you have a car accident?
你遇到车祸了吗?

7.14.

Is this the truck that hit you?
是这辆卡车撞的你吗?

7.15.

Here's my ID
这是我的身份证

7.16.

Do you need my license?
需要我的驾照吗?

7.17.

I've witnessed the accident
我目击了这场车祸

7.18.

Where's the nearest car repair shop?
最近的修车行在哪里?

7.19.

Do you have spare parts for...?
你有多余的……吗?

7.20.

Can you help me pull my car?

你能帮我拖车吗?

7.21.

Can I leave the car here?

我能把车扔在吗?

7.22.

What's wrong with my car?

我的车怎么了?

7.23.

How much is it going to cost?

要花多少钱?

7.24.

I got hit by another car; can insurance cover the cost?

我被另一辆车撞了；保险赔吗?

7.25.

It wasn't my fault at all

这不是我的错

7.26.

I was on the main road and he came from the side street

我在主路他从旁街过来

8. Car rental
租车

8.1.

I would like to rent a car
我想租一辆车

8.2.

Do you have any cars available?
你们有车吗?

8.3.

I have a reservation under the name ...
我用......的名字有预订

8.4.

I have a reservation for a small car
我预订了一辆小型车

8.5.

I'll need it for a week
我要用一个星期

8.6.

Can I get a car for the next month?
我下个月可以有一辆车吗?

8.7.

Do I need to leave you any documents?
我要给你留什么文件吗?

8.8.

How much does the renting cost?

租赁费用多少?

8.9.

What's the price per kilometer?

每公里多少钱?

8.10.

Is it manual or automatic?

它是手动档还是自动档?

8.11.

Does it take petrol or diesel?

用汽油还是柴油?

8.12.

Can you show me the controls?

能告诉我怎么控制吗?

8.13.

Does this car have central locking?

这辆车有中控锁吗?

8.14.

Does it have child locks?

它有儿童锁吗?

8.15.

Here's my driving license

这是我的驾照

8.16.

When do I need to return it?

我应该什么时候还?

8.17.

Do I have to return it with the full tank?
我必须加满油还车吗?

8.18.

Can you show me how to open the boot?
你能告诉我如何启动吗?

8.19.

Where do I turn on the lights?
我在哪里开灯?

8.20.

Where are the windscreen wipers?
雨刷在哪里?

8.21.

Can I get insurance?
我能买保险吗?

8.22.

Does the car have insurance?
这辆车有保险吗?

8.23.

Does the car have all the necessary accessories?
这辆车的配件齐全吗?

8.24.

How much do you charge if I'm an hour late?
如果我迟到一个小时你们怎么收费?

8.25.

What are your business hours?
你们的营业时间?

8.26.

Do you work on Sunday?
你们周日营业吗?

9. Car travel
汽车旅行

9.1.

I'm driving. Can you call me back?
我在开车。你能晚一会打吗?

9.2.

Can you slow down a bit?
你能稍微慢一点吗?

9.3.

Can you stop here for a moment?
你能在停一小会儿吗?

9.4.

Can we take a break here?
我们在停一会儿可以吗?

9.5.

Are we going to arrive by the evening?
我们晚上到?

9.6.

When should we arrive?
我们应该什么时候到?

9.7.

Do you know directions to ...?
你知道去......的路吗?

9.8.

Can you show me the way to ...?
你能告诉我去......的路吗?

9.9.

How do I get to the ...?
我怎么去......?

9.10.

Is there an alternative road?
有其他的路吗?

9.11.

Is there a detour or should I enter the city?
有绕道还是我要进市区?

9.12.

How can I avoid the traffic jam?
我应该怎么避免堵车?

9.13.

Are we going towards the highway?
我们去高速公路?

9.14.

Is this the right road?

是这条路吗？

9.15.

Where are you going to park?

去公园的路怎么走？

9.16.

Is this a public parking?

这是公共停车场吗**？**

9.17.

There's an empty parking lot

有一个空的停车场

9.18.

How do I pay for the parking?

我停车怎么收费**？**

9.19.

Can I go left here?

我能在左转吗**？**

9.20.

Am I allowed to go right here?

可以右转吗**？**

9.21.

Are we going left or right now?

我们应该左转还是右转**？**

9.22.

I don't know where to go on the next

intersection

我不知道下一个路口去哪里

9.23.

What's the speed limit here?

限速多少?

9.24.

What does this sign mean?

这个标志什么意思?

9.25.

Should I go over the bridge?

我应该过桥吗?

9.26.

What is the shortest way to get to the...?

去......最近的路怎么走?

9.27.

How many kilometers to...?

到......多少公里?

9.28.

Is this the way for...?

这是去......的路吗?

9.29.

Where does this road go?

这条路去哪里?

9.30.

What is the maximum speed allowed?

允许的最高速度是多少?

10. Children
孩子

10.1.

Do children need visa?

孩子需要签证吗?

10.2.

What's the children policy?

对孩子是什么政策?

10.3.

Do children get a discount?

对孩子有折扣吗?

10.4.

Do children need a separate seat?

孩子们需要单独的座位吗?

10.5.

Can I get an extra bed for a child?

我能给一个孩子单独的床吗?

10.6.

Do I need to pay the full price to get a children's seat?

我要给孩子的座位付全价吗?

10.7.

Is there a toy store nearby?

附近有玩具店吗?

10.8.

Where can I buy gifts for my children?

在哪里可以给我的孩子买礼物?

10.9.

My son is 2; does he need a ticket?

我的儿子 2 岁了；他需要买票吗?

10.10.

Is there room for pram?

有放婴儿车的地方吗?

10.11.

What do I need to sign so my child can travel without me?

我应该怎样签证我的孩子可以独立旅行?

10.12.

Here's my baby's Passport

这是我孩子的护照

10.13.

How long is the child's passport valid?

孩子的护照有效期多久?

10.14.

Do you offer any daycare service at the hotel?

你的酒店提供日间看护服务吗?

10.15.

Are there any activities for children?

有为孩子准备的活动吗?

10.16.

Where can I take my children today?

我今天能带我的孩子去哪里**?**

10.17.

I need a babysitter for few hours

我需要有人看护孩子几个小时

10.18.

Are children allowed in a restaurant?

餐馆允许孩子进入吗**?**

10.19.

Are children allowed at the event?

可以带孩子参加吗**?**

10.20.

Does the TV in our room have cartoons?

我房间里的电视可以看动画片吗**?**

11.

Cinema

电影院

11.1.

I'd like to see a movie, is there a cinema near us?

我想去看电影，我们附近有什么电影院**?**

11.2.

What's on at the cinema?

这个电影院在放什么?

11.3.

Is there anything good on at the cinema?

这个电影院有什么特别的吗?

11.4.

What's this film about?

这部电影关于什么的?

11.5.

Shall we get some popcorn?

我们来点爆米花?

11.6.

Do you want salted or sweet popcorn?

爆米花你要咸的还是甜的?

11.7.

Do you want to drink something?

你要喝点什么吗?

11.8.

Where shall we sit?

我们应该坐哪里?

11.9.

I would like to sit near the back, if possible

如果可以的话我想靠后坐

11.10.

I prefer to be near the front, if there are

available seats
如果有座位我想靠前坐

12.   Communication
交流

12.1.

Do you understand me?
你明白我的意思吗?

12.2.

Do you speak English?
你能说英语吗?

12.3.

Do you speak French?
你能说法语吗?

12.4.

Do you speak Spanish?
你能说西班牙语吗?

12.5.

Do you speak German?
你能说德语吗?

12.6.

Can you repeat that?
你能再说一次吗?

12.7.

How do you say ... in English?

英语里……怎么说**?**

12.8.

What did she say?

她说什么**?**

12.9.

What does it mean?

什么意思**?**

12.10.

Can you please translate that?

你能翻译这个吗**?**

12.11.

How do you spell it?

这个怎么拼**?**

12.12.

Can you please write that down?

你能把它写下来吗**?**

12.13.

I need to write it down. Can you please repeat?

Necesito escribirlo. ¿Me puedes repetir?

12.14.

Would you write your address here?

你能把你的地址写在吗**?**

12.15.

Can you write your phone number here?

你能把你的电话号码写在吗?

12.16.

Can I hear your email address letter by letter?

你能拼一下你的电子邮件地址吗?

12.17.

Can you send it to my email?

你能发到我的电子邮箱吗?

12.18.

Can you call him on the phone?

你能给他打电话吗?

13. Consulate
领事馆

13.1.

Where is the … consulate?

……领事馆在哪里?

13.2.

What's the number to call the consulate?

领事馆的电话号码多少?

13.3.

How do I get to the … consulate?

我怎么去……领事馆?

13.4.

Can you show me the directions to the …
consulate?

你能告诉我去......领事馆的路吗?

13.5.

Do you know the consulate address?

你知道领事馆的地址吗?

13.6.

How can I reach the consulate?

我怎么去领事馆?

13.7.

I need to speak with someone from the
consulate

我需要和领事馆的人对话

13.8.

Can I reach the consulate in case of emergency?

我在紧急情况下能去领事馆吗?

13.9.

Where's the … consulate located?

......领事馆在哪里?

14.   Customs
海关

14.1.

Do you need me to open my bag?
我需要打开我的包吗**?**

14.2.

I have nothing to declare
我没有什么要申报的

14.3.

I have some goods to declare
我有一些要申报的物品

14.4.

Do I have to pay duty on these items?
我要为这些东西支付关税吗**?**

14.5.

This is from a duty-free shop
这些是在免税商店买的

14.6.

Are you going to go through my luggage?
你要检查我的行李吗**?**

14.7.

Is this a subject to custom duty?
这个收关税吗**?**

14.8.

I have all the necessary papers for this item
我有这件东西的所有文件

14.9.

Is this an exemption from customs duty?
这个免关税吗?

14.10.

I have golden jewelry to declare
我有金首饰要申报

14.11.

These are gifts for my wife and children
这是给我妻子和孩子的礼物

14.12.

Am I allowed to bring ...?
我可以带......吗?

14.13.

I don't have any foreign currency
我没有外币

14.14.

Where is the customs clearance?
在哪里清关?

14.15.

I have the license for importing
我有进口许可证

14.16.

I paid the customs. Here's my certifícate
我付了关税。这是我的证明

15. Directions
方向

15.1.

Can you show me how to get to the … ?

你能告诉我怎么去......吗**?**

15.2.

What's the closest route to the … ?

去......最近的路线是什么**?**

15.3.

I'm headed to the … Can you help me?

我要去......你能帮助我吗**?**

15.4.

How to get to the … ?

怎么去......**?**

15.5.

I'm lost. Can you help me?

我迷路了。你能帮助我吗**?**

15.6.

I don't know which road to take. Can you help?

我不知道走哪条路。你能帮助我吗**?**

15.7.

There's no sign. Where should I go?

没有路标。我应该去哪里**?**

15.8.

I don't see any road sign, should I turn left or

right?

我没有看到路标，我应该左转还是右转**?**

15.9.

Do you have GPS?

你有 **GPS** 吗**?**

15.10.

What does the GPS say?

GPS 怎么说**?**

15.11.

Can you turn on the GPS?

你能打开 **GPS** 吗**?**

15.12.

The GPS directions aren't good, we should ask someone

GPS 的路线不好，我们应该找人问问

15.13.

Do you know how can we get to ... ?

你知道我们怎么去......吗**?**

15.14.

I'm looking for a street named ...

我在找一条叫......的街道

15.15.

Where's the number ... in this street?

这条街的......号在哪里**?**

15.16.

I need to be at the café ... in 10 minutes, where

is it?

我需要在 **10** 分钟内赶到……咖啡馆，它在哪里**?**

15.17.

Is this a one-way street?

这个是单行道吗**?**

15.18.

Will I arrive faster by car or by walking?

我坐车去还是走着去快一点**?**

15.19.

Is there a traffic jam downtown?

市区堵车吗**?**

16.   Discomfort

不适

16.1.

Can I get another seat?

我能作另外的座位吗**?**

16.2.

Can I change the departure time?

我可以改变出发时间吗**?**

16.3.

Can I open the window?

我可以开窗子吗**?**

16.4.

Can you turn up the heating?
你能把暖气打开吗?

16.5.

Can I use the restroom?
我可以用洗手间吗?

16.6.

Can I use the shower?
我可以用浴室吗?

16.7.

Can you move me to the other department?
能把我搬到其他房间吗?

16.8.

This is not what I've ordered
这不是我预订的

16.9.

This isn't fresh
这个不新鲜

16.10.

Can I speak to your manager?
我能和你的经理谈话吗?

16.11.

Can we sit in a non-smoking area?
我们能去无烟区坐吗?

16.12.

Can you please put off the cigarette?

你能把烟熄了吗**?**

16.13.

It's too cold in here

太冷了

16.14.

I can't see anything from here

我在什么都看不到

16.15.

Can you move a little bit so I can pass?

你能让一下让我过去吗**?**

16.16.

Can I cut in front of you? I only have one item

我能在你前面吗？我只有一件

16.17.

We've been here for 20 minutes. Can we order?

我们已经来了 **20** 分钟了。我们可以预约了吗**?**

16.18.

The bathroom is out of order. Is there another one?

浴室满了。有其他的吗**?**

16.19.

Excuse me, I don't feel very well

不好意思，我感觉不太好

16.20.

I'll have to go now
现在我必须走了

16.21.

I'm tired, I have to go to sleep
我累了，我必须睡觉

16.22.

I have an early meeting tomorrow, I have to leave you now
我明天有一个早会，我必须走了

16.23.

I have to go back to get my jacket
我必须回去拿我的夹克

16.24.

Do you have an extra jacket I could borrow?
你有多的夹克借我吗?

16.25.

It's raining outside; do you have a dryer?
外面下雨了；你有烘干机吗?

16.26.

Can I get a clean glass? This one has some stains
能给我一个干净的杯子吗？这个有污点

17. Embassy
大使馆

17.1.

Where is the ... embassy?

......大使馆在哪里**?**

17.2.

Do you have the embassy's number?

你有大使馆的电话吗**?**

17.3.

How do I get to the ... embassy?

我怎么去**......**大使馆**?**

17.4.

Can you show me the directions to the ... embassy?

你能告诉我去**......**大使馆的方向吗**?**

17.5.

Do you know the embassy address?

你知道大使馆的地址吗**?**

17.6.

How can I reach the embassy?

我怎么去大使馆**?**

17.7.

I need to speak with someone from the embassy

我需要和大使馆的人谈话

17.8.

Where can I see you regarding my visa status?

根据我的签证情况我能在哪里见你**?**

17.9.

Can I reach the embassy in case of emergency?

紧急情况下我能联系大使馆吗?

17.10.

Where's the ... embassy located ?

......大使馆在哪里?

18.   Gas station
加油站

18.1.

Do we need to stop for the gas?

我们要停下加油吗?

18.2.

Is there any gas station near?

附近有加油站吗?

18.3.

I'm going to be out of fuel soon

我们很快就没有燃料了

18.4.

Is oil level okay?

油充足吗?

18.5.

Do you have diesel?

你有柴油吗?

18.6.

Do you have a tire pump?

你有打气筒吗**?**

18.7.

Do you have a car wash here?

你能洗车吗**?**

18.8.

Can I wash my car?

我能洗车吗**?**

18.9.

How much does washing cost?

洗车多少钱**?**

18.10.

How much does a liter of gas cost?

一升汽油多少钱**?**

18.11.

Could you check my tires?

你能检查我的轮胎吗**?**

18.12.

Fill it up, please

请加满

18.13.

Should I go inside to pay?

我要进去付款吗**?**

18.14.

Is there a parking lot behind?
后面停的车很多吗?

18.15.

We have just passed the gas station, can we go back?
我们刚刚过了加油站，我们能回去吗?

19. Hairdresser
美发

19.1.

I'd like a haircut, please
我想剪头发

19.2.

Do I need a reservation?
我需要预定吗?

19.3.

Are you able to see me now?
你现在能看到我吗?

19.4.

Can I make an appointment for tomorrow?
我能预约明天的吗?

19.5.

Can you wash my hair?
你能给我洗头吗?

19.6.

I'd like some highlights

我想要一些造型

19.7.

Can I get a coloring?

我可以染发吗?

19.8.

I would like a blow-dry

我想用吹风机风干

19.9.

Could you trim my beard, please?

你能修剪我的胡子吗，谢谢?

19.10.

Could you trim my moustache, please?

你能修建我的小胡子吗，谢谢?

19.11.

Can you put some wax?

能打一些蜡吗?

19.12.

Can I have some gel?

能打一些胶吗?

19.13.

Please don't put any products on my hair

请不要在我的头发上用任何东西

20. Health
健康

20.1.

I'm sick, can you call a doctor?

我病了，你能叫个医生吗?

20.2.

I'm not feeling well, can you help me?

我感觉不舒服，你能帮助我吗?

20.3.

I'm nauseated, what should I do?

我感觉恶心，我应该怎么办?

20.4.

Is there any nurse?

有护士吗?

20.5.

I need a doctor urgently!

我急需一个医生!

20.6.

Where's the ER?

急诊室在哪里?

20.7.

I've got the prescription from the doctor

我有医生的处方

20.8.

Can you give me something for headache?

你能给我一些治头痛的药吗**?**

20.9.

Can you recommend anything for a cold?

你能推荐一些治感冒的药吗**?**

20.10.

Do you have any rash cream?

有皮疹药膏吗**?**

20.11.

I need something for mosquito bites

我要治蚊子叮咬的药

20.12.

Do you have anything to help me stop smoking?

你有什么可以帮助我戒烟吗**?**

20.13.

Do you have nicotine patches?

你有尼古丁贴片吗**?**

20.14.

Can I buy this without a prescription?

我没有处方可以买这个吗**?**

20.15.

Does it have any side-effects?

它有副作用吗**?**

20.16.

I'd like to speak to the pharmacist, please

我想找药剂师，谢谢

20.17.

Do you have something for sore throat?

有喉咙痛的药吗?

20.18.

Any help for chapped lips?

唇裂怎么办?

20.19.

I need cough medicine

我需要感冒药

20.20.

I feel sick when I travel, what should I do?

我旅行的时候感觉生病了，我应该怎么办?

20.21.

Can I make an appointment to see the dentist?

我可以约个时间看牙医吗?

20.22.

One of my fillings has come out, can you do something?

我的一个填料出来了，你能做些什么?

20.23.

I have a severe toothache, what should I do?

我剧烈的牙痛，应该怎么办?

20.24.

I broke a tooth, I need a dentist urgently

我断了一颗牙，我急需牙医

20.25.

My kid is not feeling well, where is the nearest ambulance?

我的孩子不舒服，最近的救护车在哪里?

20.26.

I ate something bad, I need a stomach medicine

我吃了不敢进的东西，我需要胃药

20.27.

I need an allergy medicine

我需要抗过敏药

21.   Hotel
旅馆

21.1.

Where's our hotel reservation?

我们的旅馆预约在哪里?

21.2.

Where are we going to stay?

我们在哪里过夜?

21.3.

Did you reserve the hotel?

你有预约旅馆吗?

21.4.

Did you find accommodation?
你找住宿了吗?

21.5.

Do you have the hotel address?
你有旅馆的地址吗?

21.6.

What's the hotel's phone number?
旅馆的电话号码是多少?

21.7.

Do you have my reservation?
你有我的预约吗?

21.8.

I've made the reservation under the name …
我用……的名字有预约

21.9.

My booking was for a single room
我预订了单人间

21.10.

My booking was for a double room
我预订了双人间

21.11.

My booking was for a twin room
我预订了双人间

21.12.

What is my room number?

我的房间号是多少?

21.13.

Which floor is my room on?

我的房间在几楼?

21.14.

Where can I get my keys?

我在哪里拿钥匙?

21.15.

Where are the lifts?

电梯在哪里?

21.16.

Could I have a wake-up call at seven o'clock?

可以在七点钟叫醒我吗?

21.17.

Do you lock the front door at night?

你们夜里关门吗?

21.18.

What do I do if I come back after midnight?

如果我午夜之后回来怎么办?

21.19.

Can I get my key, please?

能把钥匙给我吗?

21.20.

Do you need to know how long we're staying

for?

你需要知道我们要呆多久吗?

21.21.

Could we have an extra bed?

我们可以多要一张床吗?

21.22.

Does the room have the air condition?

房间有空调吗?

21.23.

When do you serve breakfast?

你们几点钟供应早餐?

21.24.

When is the dinner being served?

晚餐几点供应?

21.25.

Is the restaurant open?

餐厅开放吗?

21.26.

Can I conduct a meeting somewhere in the hotel?

我可以在旅馆的什么地方开会?

21.27.

Do you have a pool?

你有游泳池吗?

21.28.

Can I use the gym?

我可以用健身房吗**?**

21.29.

Are there any messages for me?

有给我的信息吗**?**

21.30.

Can we have separate rooms?

我们可以有单独的房间吗**?**

21.31.

Does the room have the mini-bar?

房间里有小冰柜吗**?**

21.32.

Is there a TV in my room?

我的房间里面有电视吗**?**

22.   Luggage

行李

22.1.

Where's my luggage?

我的行李在哪里**?**

22.2.

My luggage got lost, can you help me?

我的行李丢了，你能帮助我吗**?**

22.3.

I don't see my suitcase on the luggage conveyor

我没有在行李传送带上看到我的行李箱

22.4.

Is my bag lost?

我的包丢了**?**

22.5.

Can you help me find my luggage?

你能帮我找我的行李吗**?**

22.6.

Can someone take my luggage?

什么人拿走了我的行李**?**

22.7.

Can the bellboy help me with my luggage?

行李员能帮我拿行李吗**?**

22.8.

I can't carry all my bags, can you help me?

我拿不了我所有的包，你能帮我吗**?**

22.9.

I don't have a lot of luggage, I'll take it myself

我的行李不多，我自己拿

22.10.

I only have one bag

我只有一个包

22.11.

Please be careful, it's fragile

请小心一些，它很易碎

22.12.

I have some fragile gifts in my luggage, don't break them

我的行李里面有一些易碎的礼品，不要弄坏它们

22.13.

Can you help the lady with her luggage?

你能帮这位女士搬运行李吗?

22.14.

Where can I get a luggage cart?

我在哪里可以拿行李车?

22.15.

Where can I measure the weight of my luggage?

我在哪里称行李的重量?

22.16.

Can I repack here?

我可以在重新打包吗?

22.17.

I'm not done packing yet

我还没打包完

22.18.

Did you pack everything?

你把所有东西都打包了?

22.19.

I've finished packing, I'll wait for you outside

我打包完了，我在外面等你

22.20.

Let me help you with your bags

让我帮你拿包

22.21.

Did you put the bags in the car?

你把包放在车里?

22.22.

Help me get the luggage in the trunk

帮我从行李箱拿行李

22.23.

Keep an eye on the bags

注意包

22.24.

Can you watch my bags for a minute?

你能帮我看一会包吗?

22.25.

I need to use the bathroom. Can I leave my bag here?

我要去洗手间。我可以把包放在吗?

22.26.

Do you want me to watch your bags until you come back?

你要我在你回来之前看你的包吗?

23.   Metro travel
地铁旅行

23.1.

Where's the closest metro station?
最近的地铁站在哪里**?**

23.2.

Can I get to … with metro?
我能坐地铁去**……**吗**?**

23.3.

Where can I buy a metro ticket?
我在哪里买地铁票**?**

23.4.

How many stops are there to … ?
去**……**多少站**?**

23.5.

Do I need to make connections to go to … ?
我去**……**需要换乘吗**?**

23.6.

What's the metro ticket price?
地铁票价多少**?**

23.7.

Is there any discount for children?
孩子有折扣吗**?**

23.8.

Can you tell me when should I arrive to ... ?

能告诉我到......多久吗?

23.9.

How often does the train go?

列车多久一班?

23.10.

Should I take the metro or the bus?

我应该乘地铁还是公共汽车?

23.11.

I need to go to ... . Can metro take me there?

我要去......地铁能去吗?

23.12.

Do you have a timetable?

你有时刻表吗?

23.13.

Do you have a map for metro lines?

你有地铁线路图吗?

23.14.

Will you tell me when I get to the ...?

你能告诉我我什么时候到……吗?

24.   Money

钱

24.1.

Have you got the money?

你拿到钱了吗?

24.2.

I forgot the money, I need to go back

我忘了拿钱，我需要回去

24.3.

I have the money here

我有钱

24.4.

Do we have enough money?

我们的钱够吗?

24.5.

How much cash do we need?

我们需要多少现金?

24.6.

Can I pay in cash?

我可以用现金支付吗?

24.7.

Can I pay with credit card?

我可以用信用卡支付吗?

24.8.

Where's the closest ATM?

最近的自动柜员机在哪里?

24.9.

I need to get some cash for tonight

我今晚需要一些现金

24.10.

The bill is covered

账单付过了

24.11.

I'll pay for everything

我会支付所有的

24.12.

Please let me pay the bill

请让我付账

24.13.

Can we split the bill?

我们可以分开付吗**?**

24.14.

How much do I owe you?

我欠你多少**?**

24.15.

Let me get my wallet

让我拿我的钱包

24.16.

My wallet is in the car, I'll be right back

我的钱包在车里，我马上就回来

24.17.

There are no ATMs here
这里没有自动柜员机

24.18.

Can you lend me some money until tomorrow?
你能借我些钱到明天吗**?**

24.19.

Can I write you a check?
我可以给你签支票吗**?**

24.20.

Can you accept my Visa card?
你能接受我的维萨卡吗**?**

24.21.

Is there any problem with my card?
我的卡有问题吗**?**

24.22.

Can I check my account balance?
我可以查我的帐户余额吗**?**

24.23.

I need to get to the bank right now
我需要马上去银行

24.24.

I have a problem regarding money
我有个关于钱的问题

24.25.

I'd like to withdraw some money
我想取一些钱

25.   Passport
护照

25.1.

Do you need to check our passports?
你需要检查我们的护照吗?

25.2.

Is my passport valid?
我的护照有效吗?

25.3.

Where did you put our passports?
你把我们的护照放在哪里了?

25.4.

I lost my passport. What should I do?
我丢了我的护照。我应该怎么办?

25.5.

My passport expired. What should I do?
我的护照过期了。我应该怎么办?

25.6.

When can I expect my passport to be ready?
我的护照什么时候能好?

25.7.

Could I see your passport?

我可以看一下你的护照吗**?**

25.8.

My passport is in my pocket, where is yours?

我的护照在我的口袋里，你的呢**?**

25.9.

How long will my passport be valid?

我的护照有效期多久**?**

25.10.

Where is the passport control?

检查护照的地方在哪里**?**

25.11.

Do I need to go through passport control?

我需要穿过检查护照的地方吗**?**

25.12.

Do little children need their own passports?

小孩子需要他们自己的护照吗**?**

25.13.

Make sure you always know where your passport is

确保你始终知道你的护照在哪里

25.14.

It's the best to keep the passport on hand

最好把护照拿在手里

25.15.

What number should I call if I lose my passport?

如果我丢了护照我应该打哪个号码?

25.16.

If I lose my passport, should I go to the embassy?

如果我丢了护照，我应该去大使馆吗?

25.17.

We're traveling together; here are our passports

我们在一起旅行；这是我们的护照

25.18.

What happens if my passport expires while I'm abroad?

如果我在国外的时候护照过期会怎么样?

25.19.

I have a question regarding my passport status

我有个关于我的护照情况的问题

25.20.

Where can I travel with my passport?

我的护照可以去哪里?

25.21.

Is just a passport enough?

只有护照就够了吗?

25.22.

Do I need anything else besides passport?

除了护照我还需要别的什么**?**

25.23.

Can I get my passport back?

我能拿回我的护照吗**?**

25.24.

Do I need to show my passport on the airport?

在机场需要出示我的护照吗**?**

25.25.

Do I need the passport for traveling to … ?

去**......**需要护照吗**?**

25.26.

Can you help me find my passport? It's here somewhere

你能帮我找我的护照吗？它在这里的某个地方

26.   Personal accidents
   人身伤害

26.1.

I'm hurt, I need help

我受伤了，我需要帮助

26.2.

My foot is stuck, can you help me?

窝的脚被卡住了，你能帮助我吗？

26.3.

I've hurt my arm

我的胳膊受伤了

26.4.

Here's where it hurts

这是受伤的地方

26.5.

Call the fire department

打电话给消防队

26.6.

The hotel is on fire, hurry up

旅馆着火吗，快点

26.7.

Do you know CPR?

你懂心脏复苏术吗?

26.8.

I need a hospital urgently

我需要赶紧去医院

26.9.

The thief just attacked me, call the police

小偷袭击了我，叫警察

26.10.

They took all my money and documents

他们拿走了我所有的钱和文件

26.11.

Please block my credit card, it's been stolen

请锁定我的信用卡，它被偷了

26.12.

Where is the police station?

警察局在哪里？

26.13.

It's an emergency

情况紧急

26.14.

Is the fire department on their way?

消防队来了没有？

26.15.

I've been robbed, call the police

我被抢劫了，叫警察

26.16.

He's the thief

他是那个贼

26.17.

He stole my wallet

他偷了我的钱包

27. Personal information
个人信息

27.1.

What's your last name?
你姓什么?

27.2.

Can I get your phone number?
能告诉我你的电话号码吗?

27.3.

Can I get your business card?
能给我你的名片吗?

27.4.

Here's my card with all the information
这是我的名片所有信息都在上面

27.5.

What's your email address?
你的电子邮箱地址是?

27.6.

Where are you from?
你从哪里来?

27.7.

Where do you live?
你住在哪里?

27.8.

Can I get your address?
能告诉我你的地址吗?

27.9.

What's your room number?

你的房间号是多少?

27.10.

Are you married?

你结婚了吗?

27.11.

Do you have children?

你有孩子吗?

27.12.

Can I call you if I need you?

需要的话我可以给你打电话吗?

27.13.

Can I count on you to send me that? Here's my address

你能把它寄给我吗？这是我的地址

28. Phone

电话

28.1.

Can I call you later?

我可以给你打电话吗?

28.2.

Here's my phone number

这是我的电话号码

28.3.

You can reach me on this number

你可以用这个号码联系我

28.4.

Do you have his phone number?

你有他的电话号码吗?

28.5.

Where can I get emergency numbers for the country I'm going to?

在我去的国家我在哪里能找到紧急电话?

28.6.

What's the number for the police?

报警电话号码是多少?

28.7.

What's the number for the ambulance?

急救电话号码是多少?

28.8.

What's the number for the fire department?

消防队电话号码是多少?

28.9.

How can I reach the hotel?

我怎么样去旅馆?

28.10.

Have you written down the hotel's phone number?

你记下旅馆的电话号码了吗?

28.11.

Is this the number for the airport?

这个是机场的电话号码吗**?**

28.12.

Hello, can I speak to …?

你好，我想找**……?**

28.13.

I need to speak to …, do I have the right number?

我想找**……**，我没打错吧**?**

28.14.

Can I call you again? The signal is bad

我能再打给你吗？信号不好

28.15.

I'm afraid you have the wrong number

恐怕你打错了

28.16.

Can I leave a message for … ?

我能给**……**留言吗**?**

28.17.

Can you tell him to call me?

能告诉他给我打电话吗**?**

28.18.

Please don't call me after 9pm

晚上 **9** 点之后不要给我打电话

28.19.

You won't be able to reach me during the weekend

你周末找不到我的

28.20.

Would you give me your phone number so I can call you tomorrow?

你能给我你的电话号码吗，这样我明天可以给你打电话?

28.21.

My phone will be unavailable for the next week

我的电话下周会无法接通

28.22.

Write me an email instead

给我发电子邮件代替

28.23.

It seems like I've lost your number

看起来我丢了你的号码

28.24.

I couldn't reach you this morning, what's going on?

今天上午我联系不到你，怎么了?

28.25.

My battery is going to die, do you have a charger?

我的电池没电了，你有充电器吗?

28.26.

Can I charge my phone here?
我能在这里给我的手机充电吗**?**

29. **Plane and airport**
飞机和机场

29.1.

I've got a ticket to ...
我有去**......**的票

29.2.

Where can I check my ticket?
我在哪里检票**?**

29.3.

I only have a carry on
我只有一件行李

29.4.

I have 2 suitcases, can I check them now?
我有两个行李箱，现在我可以检查它们吗**?**

29.5.

What is the maximum luggage weight?
最大的行李重量多少**?**

29.6.

I would like to confirm my flight
我想确认我的航班

29.7.

Can you confirm my ticket number?

你能确认我的机票号码吗?

29.8.

Can I get the window seat?

我能要靠窗的座位吗?

29.9.

Can I get the aisle seat?

我能要靠走道的座位吗?

29.10.

I have a ticket; can I schedule a departure date?

我有一张票；我能安排离去的日期吗?

29.11.

Can I change my departure date to ... ?

我能把我的离开日期改成......吗?

29.12.

I would like to leave on ... , if there are available seats

如果有作为的话，我想......走

29.13.

Would my bag fit over the seat?

我的包适合放到座位上吗?

29.14.

Can I have a seat closest to the emergency exit?

我能要最靠近紧急出口的座位吗?

29.15.

Which gate do I need to go to?

我需要走哪个门**?**

29.16.

What is the gate number?

门的号码是什么**?**

29.17.

Can you point me towards the gate?

你能指给我那个门吗**?**

29.18.

How do I get to the gate?

我怎么去那个门**?**

29.19.

When should I be at the gate?

我应该什么时候到那个门**?**

29.20.

I'm looking for the north terminal.

我在找北出口

29.21.

Where can I claim my luggage?

我在哪里领行李**?**

29.22.

Could you please help me with my bags?

你能帮我拿一下包吗**?**

29.23.

Can you repeat the flight number?
你能再说一遍航班号吗?

29.24.

Here's my passport and boarding card
这是我的护照和登机牌

29.25.

Will there be a delay?
会晚点吗?

29.26.

How long does the flight take?
要飞多久?

29.27.

Do you serve food and drinks?
你提供食物和饮料吗?

29.28.

Can I unfasten my seatbelt now?
现在我可以解开安全带吗?

30. Professions
职业

30.1.

I'm a lawyer
我是律师

30.2.

Are you a nurse?

你是护士吗?

30.3.

So, he's an executive?

所以，他是个高管?

30.4.

We need an electrician

我们需要一个电工

30.5.

I could use a hairdresser now

现在我需要一 个美发师

30.6.

Are you an engineer, too?

你也是工程师吗?

30.7.

Do you work as a librarian?

你是图书管理员吗?

30.8.

Is he a famous actor?

他是著名演员吗?

30.9.

This tailor is really good

这个裁缝真的很好

30.10.

I'll take you to the doctor

我会带你去看医生

30.11.

Do you know some good mechanist?

你认识好的机械师吗?

30.12.

Is there any reliable butcher near?

附近有好的屠夫吗?

30.13.

I need to see a dentist today

我今天需要看牙医

30.14.

What is your occupation?

你做什么职业?

30.15.

Where do you work?

你在哪里工作?

31.   Restaurant
餐馆

31.1.

Do you know any good restaurants?

你知道什么好的餐馆吗?

31.2.

Where's the nearest restaurant?

最近的餐馆在哪里?

31.3.

Would you join me for lunch?

我们一起吃午餐吧?

31.4.

Be my guest for dinner tonight

今晚我请你吃晚餐

31.5.

Do you have any free tables?

你有空桌子吗?

31.6.

A table for four, please

四个人的桌子，谢谢

31.7.

I'd like to make a reservation

我想预约

31.8.

I'd like to book a table, please

我想订一张桌子，谢谢

31.9.

Tonight at ... o'clock

今晚......点

31.10.

Tomorrow at ... o'clock

明天......点

31.11.

I've got a reservation under the name ...

我用......的名字有预约

31.12.

Could I see the menu, please?

我能看一下菜谱吗，谢谢**?**

31.13.

Can we get something to drink?

我们能要一些饮料吗**?**

31.14.

Can we order now?

现在我们可以点餐了吗**?**

31.15.

Do you have any specials?

你们有什么特色**?**

31.16.

What's the soup of the day?

今天有什么汤**?**

31.17.

What do you recommend?

你有什么推荐**?**

31.18.

What's this dish?

这是什么菜?

31.19.

I'm allergic to ...

我对……过敏

31.20.

I'm a vegetarian, what do you recommend?

我是素食者，你有什么推荐的?

31.21.

I'd like my stake medium-rare

我想要半生的牛排

31.22.

I prefer the stake to be well done

我想要熟的牛排

31.23.

We're in a hurry, when can we be served?

我们赶时间，什么时候能上菜?

31.24.

How long will it take?

要等多久?

31.25.

What is your wine selection?

你喝什么酒?

31.26.

Do you have any desserts?

你有什么甜点?

31.27.

Could I see the dessert menu?

我能看一下甜点菜单吗?

31.28.

Can you take this back, it's cold

你能把这个带回去吗, 太冷了

31.29.

Can I get the new serving, this is too salty

我能再要一份吗, 这个太咸了

31.30.

This doesn't taste right, can I change my order?

这个吃起来不好, 我能改我菜吗?

31.31.

We've been waiting a long time, can you help us?

我们已经等了很久了, 你能帮我们吗?

31.32.

Is our meal on its way?

我们的饭做了没有?

31.33.

Will our food be long?

我们的食物要等很久吗?

31.34.

Could we have the bill, please?

我们能看一下账单吗，谢谢**?**

31.35.

Do you take credit cards?

你可以收信用卡吗**?**

31.36.

Can we pay separately?

我们可以分开付吗**?**

31.37.

Please bring us another bottle of wine

请再给我们一瓶酒

31.38.

Please bring us some more bread

请给我们多拿一些面包

31.39.

Can we have a jug of tap water?

能给我们一壶白开水吗**?**

31.40.

Can I have some water, please?

能给我一些水吗，谢谢**?**

31.41.

What kind of meat is this?

这是什么肉**?**

31.42.

How do you prepare the pork?
你们怎么做猪肉?

31.43.

I'm allergic to nuts, please don't put them in
我对坚果过敏，不要放坚果

31.44.

Sorry, but I suffer from allergy from shellfish
不好意思，我对贝类过敏

31.45.

Do you have chicken breasts?
你有鸡胸吗?

31.46.

Have you got roasted turkey?
你有烤火鸡吗?

31.47.

I'll have the roast beef, please
我要烤牛肉，谢谢

31.48.

What's your pasta selection?
你要什么意大利面?

31.49.

What kind of beans do you serve?
你们提供什么豆子?

31.50.

Can I get the salt?

我能要盐吗?

31.51.

Could you pass the pepper?

你能递一下胡椒吗?

31.52.

Can you bring the olive oil?

你能把橄榄油拿过来吗?

31.53.

Can you put vinegar in the salad?

你能在沙拉里放醋吗?

31.54.

Do you have any seafood?

你们有海鲜吗?

31.55.

I'll have bacon and eggs

我想要火腿和鸡蛋

31.56.

Can I get some sausages?

我能要一些香肠吗?

31.57.

Do you serve fried chicken?

你们有炸鸡吗?

31.58.

I'll have baked potatoes with that

我想要烤土豆和那一起

31.59.

Can I order some grilled chicken?

我能要一些烤鸡吗?

31.60.

I'll have a piece of chocolate cake

我想要一块巧克力蛋糕

31.61.

I'll have ice cream for a desert

我想要冰淇淋作为甜点

31.62.

Croissant and coffee, please

羊角面包和咖啡，谢谢

31.63.

Two pancakes with honey for me

给我两个蜂蜜煎饼

31.64.

Is smoking allowed?

可以抽烟吗?

32. Supermarket
超市

32.1.

What times are you open?
你们几点开门?

32.2.

Are you open on Saturday?
你们星期六营业吗?

32.3.

Do you work on Sunday?
你们星期日营业吗?

32.4.

What time do you close today?
今天几点钟关门?

32.5.

What time do you open tomorrow?
你们明天几点开门?

32.6.

How much is this?
这个多少钱?

32.7.

How much does this cost?
这个多少钱?

32.8.

I'll pay in cash
我付现金

32.9.

Do you accept credit cards?

你们可以刷信用卡吗?

32.10.

Could I have a receipt, please?

能给我一张收据吗，谢谢?

32.11.

Could you tell me where the ... is?

你能告诉我......在哪里吗?

32.12.

Could I have a carrier bag, please?

我能要一个购物袋吗，谢谢?

32.13.

Can you help me pack my groceries?

你能帮我包装杂货吗?

32.14.

Here's my loyalty card

这是我的优惠卡

32.15.

Where can I find milk?

牛奶在哪里?

32.16.

What kind of bread should we buy?

我们应该买什么样的面包?

32.17.

Could you tell me where the meat section is?

你能告诉我肉类区在哪里吗?

32.18.

Where can I find the frozen food?

冷冻食品在哪里?

32.19.

I would like some cheese, please

我想要一些奶酪，谢谢

32.20.

Do you have frozen pizza?

你们有冷冻的披萨吗?

32.21.

I want to buy some ham

我想买些火腿

32.22.

Do you have black olives?

你们有黑橄榄吗?

32.23.

I need some bottled water

我需要一些瓶装水

32.24.

We need orange juice

我们需要桔子汁

32.25.

Please show me where's the fruit aisle

请告诉我水果走道在哪里

32.26.

What vegetables do we need for the salad?

我们做沙拉需要什么蔬菜?

32.27.

Can I get some chicken wings?

我能买一下鸡翅吗?

33. Taxi

出租车

33.1.

Do you know where I can get a taxi?

你知道我在哪儿打出租车吗?

33.2.

Do you have a taxi number?

你有出租车的电话吗?

33.3.

I need the taxi. My address is ...

我需要出租车。我的地址是……

33.4.

Do you have an available vehicle right now?

你现在有可用的车吗?

33.5.

I'm at the ... street

我在......街道

33.6.

I'll wait in front of the post office on ... street?

我在......街道的邮局门口等

33.7.

How long will I have to wait?

我要等多久**?**

33.8.

Can you send a larger vehicle?

你能派一辆大一点的车吗**?**

33.9.

I'd like to go to ...

我想去......

33.10.

Could you take me to ...?

你能带我去......吗**?**

33.11.

I need to be at the airport in 30 minutes

我要在 **30** 分钟之内到机场

33.12.

I have a train in 40 minutes, please hurry

我 **40** 分钟以后坐火车，请快一点

33.13.

Try to avoid the jam
试着不要堵车

33.14.

Can you put my bags in the trunk?
你能把我的包放到行李箱里吗?

33.15.

How long will the journey take?
路上要多长时间?

33.16.

Do you mind if I open the window?
我可以打开窗户吗?

33.17.

Can you please close the window?
你能把窗户关上吗?

33.18.

Are we almost there?
我们快到了吗?

33.19.

Can you hurry up?
你能快一点吗?

33.20.

That's fine, keep the change
很好，不用找零了

33.21.

Could I have a receipt, please?

能给我一张收据吗，谢谢**?**

33.22.

Could you pick me up here tonight at ...?

你今晚**......**能在这里接我吗**?**

33.23.

Could you wait for me here?

你能在等我吗**?**

33.24.

How much do you charge waiting?

你等待的话收费多少**?**

33.25.

Can you stop in front of the pharmacy?

你能在药店前面停车吗**?**

33.26.

Please take me downtown

带我去市中心

33.27.

Drive me to the theatre...

带我去剧院**......**

34. Theatre
剧院

34.1.

Is the theatre in this town any good?

这个城市的剧院有什么特别的吗?

34.2.

What's on the repertoire for this week?

本周的曲目是什么?

34.3.

Is there anything on at the theatre this week?

这周剧院在演什么?

34.4.

Any interesting plays this month?

这个月有什么有趣的上演吗?

34.5.

Do you know is there any play tonight?

你知道今晚有什么演出吗?

34.6.

When's does the play start?

演出什么时间开始?

34.7.

Does anyone I might have heard of in the play?

参加演出的有什么我知道的人吗?

34.8.

What type of production is it?

它是什么类型的作品?

34.9.

What time does the performance start?

表演几点开始?

34.10.

What time does it finish?

几点结束?

34.11.

Where's the cloakroom?

盥洗室在哪里?

34.12.

Could I have a program, please?

能给我一张节目表吗，谢谢?

34.13.

Shall we order some drinks for the interval?

我们应该点一些饮料间隔时喝吗?

34.14.

We'd better go back to our seats, it's starting

我们最好回到我们的座位上，它开始了

34.15.

Shall we sit on a balcony?

我们应该坐在阳台上?

34.16.

Check the tickets for our seat numbers

看一下票上我们的座位编号

35. Time and date
时间和日期

35.1.

What time is it?
现在几点钟?

35.2.

What date is it today?
今天几号?

35.3.

I'll be there around three-fifteen
我大约三刻钟到那里

35.4.

It's half past five, let's meet in an hour
现在是五点半，我们一个小时内见面

35.5.

I'll be there around two o'clock
我大约两点钟左右到那里

35.6.

Expect me around quarter to four
我大概三点四十五到

35.7.

Please arrive on time
请准时到达

35.8.

When did you meet him?

你什么时候和他见面**?**

35.9.

Should I come back in thirty minutes?

我应该在三十分钟之内回来**?**

35.10.

Which day is it?

是哪一天**?**

35.11.

I've been there for a few months

He estado allí por unos cuantos meses

35.12.

Can I see you later this month?

这个月晚些时候我能见到你吗**?**

35.13.

I remember you. Were you here last year?

我记得你。你去年在**?**

35.14.

I won't be available until next month

下个月之前我都没时间

35.15.

Is it always this crowded on/ the weekends?

**¿Siempre está así de lleno/ en el fin de
semana?**

35.16.

Talk to you tomorrow morning

明天早上和你说

35.17.

I'll probably be back in a few days

我大概几天之后回来

35.18.

I've been waiting for a whole hour

我已经等了整整一个小时

35.19.

I met him last Friday

我上个周五见过他

35.20.

When can I expect you?

我什么时候能见到你?

35.21.

I'll come on Wednesday

我周三到

35.22.

What are your plans for the winter?

你冬天准备去干什么?

36. Train travel
乘坐列车

36.1.

Can I get a first class single ticket?

我想要一张一等座单程票。

36.2.

Give me two first class return tickets

给我两张一等座的返程票

36.3.

I would like a child single

我想要一张儿童单程票

36.4.

I need one child return

我要一张儿童返程票

36.5.

What time's the next train to ...?

下一班去......的车是几点钟**?**

36.6.

Can I buy a ticket on the train?

我能在列车上买票吗**?**

36.7.

How much is a first class return to ...?

回......的头等票多少钱**?**

36.8.

Which platform do I need for ...?

去......在哪个站台**?**

36.9.

Is this the right platform for ...?

这是去......的站台吗?

36.10.

Where can I see the timetable?

我在哪里能看到时刻表?

36.11.

How often do the trains run to ...?

去......的列车多长时间一班?

36.12.

I'd like to renew my season ticket, please

我想更新我的季票，谢谢

36.13.

The train's running late

列车晚点了

36.14.

The train's been cancelled

列车取消了

36.15.

Does this train stop at ...?

这趟列车在......停吗?

36.16.

Is there a buffet car on the train?

列车上有餐车吗?

36.17.

Do you mind if I open the window?

我开窗可以吗**?**

36.18.

Does this train terminate here?

这趟列车的终点站是这里**?**

36.19.

Where should I put my personal belongings?

我应该把我的个人财务放在哪里**?**

36.20.

How many stops is it to …?

到**……**有多少站**?**

36.21.

How much is the ticket to …?

到**……**的票多少钱**?**

36.22.

Is there a reduced fare for children?

孩子有优惠票价吗**?**

36.23.

Is there a reduced fare for large families?

大家庭有优惠票价吗**?**

36.24.

Where is the train station?

车站在哪里**?**

36.25.

Where can we buy tickets?

我们在哪里买票?

36.26.

What time will the train to ... leave?

到......的列车几点开?

36.27.

Where is platform number ...?

......号站台在哪里?

37. Visa

签证

37.1.

Do I need a visa to go to...?

我去......需要签证吗?

37.2.

I don't have a visa. Can I still go to...?

我没有签证。我仍然可以......吗?

37.3.

I need a visa for ... . What should I do?

我需要一个......签证我应该怎么做?

37.4.

When is my visa expiring?

我的签证什么时候到期?

37.5.

Can I stay for a month with this visa?

拿这个签证我能呆一个月吗**?**

37.6.

Which documents do I need to get a visa?

拿签证需要什么文件**?**

37.7.

Is my visa ready?

我的签证好了吗**?**

37.8.

When can I get the visa?

我什么时候能拿到签证**?**

37.9.

I need a tourist visa, what should I do?

我想要一个旅游签证，应该怎么做**?**

37.10.

Who should I talk to about visa extension?

¿A quién le debo hablar para una extensión de la visa?

37.11.

Do kids need visas?

孩子需要签证吗**?**

37.12.

What will happen if our visa expires?

我们的签证过期了会怎么样**?**

37.13.

How long does the tourist visa last?
旅游签证有效期多久?

37.14.

I need a work visa for United States
我需要一个美国的工作签证

37.15.

Which countries can I go to without visa?
有哪些国家我不需要签证就可以去的?

37.16.

When can I expect your call regarding my visa status?
我什么时候能接到你的电话关于我的签证状态?

37.17.

Is this the paper that confirms that I have visa?
这是我签证的确认文件吗?

37.18.

How long does the process of getting visa last?
拿到签证的过程要多久?

37.19.

Do I need anything else besides visa?
除了签证我还需要别的什么吗?

37.20.

Am I going to need a letter of guarantee or just a visa?
我需要担保信还是只需要签证?

38. Weather
天气

38.1.

What's the weather like there?

那里的天气怎么样**?**

38.2.

Is it going to rain next week?

下周会下雨吗**?**

38.3.

Do you think there will be snow?

你认为那里会下雪吗**?**

38.4.

Can I expect sunny vacation?

我能期待一个阳光的旅途吗**?**

38.5.

I'm going with the car. Is there any fog?

我开这辆车去。有雾吗**?**

38.6.

Will the weather affect my flight?

天气会影响我的航班吗**?**

38.7.

Are we still going if it starts snowing?

如果开始下雪了我们还去吗**?**

38.8.

Is there any snow on the mountains?
山上有雪吗?

38.9.

Are we going to be able to go skiing?
我们能去滑冰吗?

38.10.

Is it warm enough for swimming?
那里温暖的足够游泳吗?

38.11.

Will it still rain tomorrow?
明天还会下雨吗?

38.12.

What's the forecast for ...?
......的天气预报怎么说?

38.13.

Do you think we'll arrive on time with this storm?
你认为在这场暴风雨之中我们会准时到达吗?

38.14.

Do I need the winter clothes?
我需要冬天的衣服吗?

38.15.

Should I pack some warm shoes?
我应该打包一些暖和的鞋子吗?

38.16.

Should I bring the jacket?

我应该带这件夹克吗**?**

38.17.

Are you expecting bad weather in the next 10 days?

你认为在接下来的 **10** 天里天气会很糟糕吗**?**

38.18.

It's really cloudy; do you think it will rain tonight?

云好多，你认为今天晚上会下雨吗**?**

37525244R00066